Where to Begin:
Selected Letters of Cid Corman and Mike Doyle
1967-1970

SENDER'S NAME AND ADDRESS — NOM ET ADRESSE DE L'ENVOYEUR

Doyle
759 Helvetia Cres.
Victoria, B.C.
Canada

NO ENCLOSURE PERMITTED — NE RIEN INSÉRER
POSTES CANADA POST

SECOND FOLD HERE — PLIER ENSUITE ICI

AIR
MAIL

PAR
AVION

AEROGRAMME

VICTORIA
6 PM
AUG 4
1969
B.C.

SPEED DELIVE
10¢
CANADA
POSTES POSTAGE

Cid Corman,
Fukuoji-cho 82, Utano,
Ukyo-ku, Kyoto 616,
JAPAN

Where to Begin:

Selected Letters of
Cid Corman and Mike Doyle
1967-1970

Edited by Kegan Doyle

Ekstasis  Editions

Canadian Cataloguing in Publication Data

Doyle, Mike
        Where to begin.

        ISBN 1-896860-74-5

                1. Doyle, Mike, 1928-- Corresponden ce. 2. Corman,
Cid--Correspondence. 3. Poets, Canadian (English)--20th century--
Correspondence.* 4. Poets, American--20th century--Corespon-
dence. Corma, Cid. II. Doyle, Kegan, 1964--   III. Title.
        Ps8557.O9Z52   2000   C811'.54   C00-911O91-7
        PR9199.3.D64Z483   2000

Introduction © Kegan Doyle, 2000.
Letters © Mike Doyle, Cid Corman, 2000.

Published in 2000 by:
Ekstasis Editions Canada Ltd.
Box 8474, Main Postal Outlet   Ekstasis Editions
Victoria, B.C. V8W 3S1   Box 571
                                          Banff, Alberta ToL oCu

THE CANADA COUNCIL | LE CONSEIL DES ARTS
        FOR THE ARTS | DU CANADA
            SINCE 1957 | DEPUIS 1957

Where to Begin: Selected Letters of Cid Corman and Mike Doyle, 1969-1970 has been
published with the assistance of a grant from the Canada Council and the Cultural
Services Branch of British Columbia.

Introduction

In mid-1967, Mike Doyle, then spending a year as a Visiting Fellow in American Studies at Yale University, first wrote to Cid Corman at his home in Kyoto, Japan. Doyle was in the early stages of a study that would eventually become **William Carlos Williams and the American Poem** (1982), and wrote to Corman as a consequence of reading 'On Measure: A Statement for Cid Corman' in Williams' **Selected Essays**. The correspondence which followed continued substantially until 1974, and thereafter sporadically. The letters included here are an edited selection from 1967 until late 1970, when the two first met at the University of Victoria where Corman gave a reading with Doyle as host.

For the first year, only Corman's side of the correspondence is available, but the relationship of the two poets, with Corman as mentor and adviser, is clear, as are the questions raised, some of them personal. The main purpose of the present selection is to show Corman in his relation to poetry, as poet, editor, and adviser, his concerns about education, and personal psychology.

Corman was born in Boston in 1924. After attending Tufts University and elsewhere, he moved around the United States, returning to Boston in 1949, where he began hosting a radio show on WMEX in Boston, called 'This is Poetry.' Designed to expose the public to contemporary poetry, the program also exposed Corman to several of American poetry's young lights and aging stars, including Robert Creeley and Marianne Moore. In 1950, Corman had contact with two men who would influence his poetry and poetics: William Carlos Williams and Charles Olson. The following year he launched the poetry journal Origin, which, by publishing Olson and Creeley, as well as Louis Zukofsky, and the French poet Francis Ponge among others, helped transform American poetry. Corman has continued to publish Origin since moving to Japan in the early sixties, in separate series usually of twenty numbers. Crucial to understanding the early years of Origin is the correspondence of Olson and Corman. As mentor and collaborator, Olson was passionate, but also difficult and at times domineering. When in the present letters one hears Corman sounding harsh with Doyle, one can almost hear the voice of Olson in the background, chiding the younger Corman. Although Corman has not achieved the fame of Olson or Creeley, his numerous volumes of poetry which include **Livingdying**, **Plight**, **Of**, have made him an underground cult figure with a substantial following. His poems are of a special purity and in their own way defy critical comment.

Charles (later Mike) Doyle was born in Birmingham in 1928. He lived and wrote in New Zealand for many years, but in 1968 he moved with his family to Victoria, B.C. In the period covered by the letters below, he was an interested follower of the Black Mountain movement, though his temperament as a poet never found it fully congenial. He did, however, learn a great deal from that association, much of it through Corman, and was thus influenced as editor of the small poetry journal Tuatara, which ran for twelve issues from 1969 until 1974. Among other things, **Tuatara** was one of the first journals to publish Ron Silliman, Bruce Andrews and Charles Bernstein and other L=A=N=G=U=A=G=E poets.

From the letters below, it will appear that a personal regard developed between the two writers and Corman had much of interest and value to impart concerning contemporary poetry. While Doyle learned a great deal about the economy of poetry, in the long run his needs and temperament led him to a more directly personal and perhaps more apparently rhetorical kind of utterance. I have ended this selection in the Fall of 1970 when Corman and his wife, Shizumi, were Doyle's guests in Victoria for a week or so. Corman's visit, the first and only meeting of the two poets, was his first trip to North America for many years and was part of an extensive reading tour of the United States and Canada.

I have left both writers' idiosyncrasies of punctuation and spelling intact, save for when clarity was at stake or I felt something was an 'accidental.' I have not tampered with Corman's habit of not using apostrophes. Both Corman and Doyle refer to other writers using initials. Generally, it is obvious who is being referred to. I have also provided a short index of names at the back of the book.

I would like to thank both Cid Corman and Mike Doyle for their generous support of this project.

Kegan Doyle

Letter 1

Utano
11th June 1967

Dear Charles,

well, let's see where to begin.

I've printed some of my correspondence of that time with W[illiam]C[arlos]W[illiams]—the "frame" of the ON MEASURE essay. For just such interested people as yourself.

I have, frankly, no use for ANY critical terminology. WCW's poetry remains alive for me, especially the later poems as well as those from SPRING & ALL. but the development OUT is via Zukofsky.

Your own two pieces ARE thin, I'm sorry to say. And a lot of it is just the kind of rhetoric I'm alluding to—though outwardly you 'play' it like WCW. 'time's shifting kaleidoscope'! Come on now. It is a matter of language—whether you (impersonal) like it or not. And very much as Bill put it. Not much I can do for you or anyone in this regard, but a personal breakthru is required, clearly. And it cant be done by teaching at a U.

Yours,

Cid Corman

LETTER 2

Utano
20th June 1967

Dear Charles,

good to have a clear and open response from you. More often than not such a letter as I wrote you draws venom. But that's the risk in saying anything these days, or trying to.

LZ (Zukofsky) provides the greatest profit in terms of the art today—in English—and also the greatest delight. The oeuvre is considerable and it is worth pondering that his work—which has been steady for over 40 years and fine at every point—has been so thoroughly neglected, studiously overlooked. However, many younger poets are finding him and that bodes well—or better. His essays are being published in London now (Rapp & Carroll) under the title of PREPOSITIONS and are well worth reading and reflecting on. He is much sharper than WCW, has more intellectual depth and a finer ear and his work has more variety and richness than seems possible for one man to have. It has a lot of 'play' to it and an immense vocabulary.

Yes, your own ear and sense of language will and must predominate. But again all the poems you send along are, for me 'exercises' at most. It is the sort of work that risks no life. It is literary, wordy, academic. I'm not interested, of course, in hurting your feelings, etc. It is poetry that concerns me and I sense from your letter that we are in agreement in this. I hope so. Words that keep saying: Look, ma, I'm dancing! I.e., See how clever your boy is—everybody! bore me silly. You have to cut away all that encrusted crud that satisfying 'professors' accomplishes. You cant MOVE in such armor. You have to come out where the tides are and where it takes breath you havent got—to go. Dont try to say so much, but say precisely what you know, know from the fulness of feeling and damn the language. I dont mean mere 'spill'. I mean setting it down clearly, cleanly, with absolute economy and simplicity, and with such accuracy that it sings, must sing.

Try living via your poetry and you may be forced into making poetry that is alive. Is a living. The anti-stands are less valuable, to me, than the pro-stands. And most people I've met who profess to be against war are unusually violent and noisy souls. But I am willing to believe it is deeper than that with you.

Yours— always,

Cid


```
3/Do you know
  what it is
  to be dead?

  But of course
  you do.  Is
  there any

  thing else in
  fact we do
  ever know?
```

Love to the family always — [signature]

Letter 3

Utano
1st July 1967

Dear Charles,

you're a glutton. OK.

Your ABANDONED SOFA' is ok and the others 'begin'. but keep it to what is really GOING--not mere repetition. Nor do I mean—as some people no doubt imagine—that everyone should be writing haiku or tanka or whathaveyou. Anyhow, one day, when you have had time to get into LZ enough—and his oeuvre is considerable, though there may not be, as yet, more than 6-10 of us who have seen and sounded it thru, all of which is worth experiencing. Get the other volume of ALL, then 'A' 1-12 in the Jonathan Cape reprint of the edition I did here a number of years ago, my major claim to fame someday, I daresay.

I's , of course, is a sequence of short pieces—independent, by and large, but with the same modus operandi—as the title cues you (us). (I'm only saying what I see.) LZ points up the SOUNDING of a poem—and he is remarkably unpredictable while proving—gradually—unexpectedly convincing. (His 'A'-18 is to appear in the August issue of POETRY he writes me and you should watch for that and pick up back issues of earlier sections that follow *'A'-12*.)

What you say seems reasonable to me. but there is a lot more play to poetry than what you seem to want to confine 'emotional charge' to. I like much of WCW that has very little of that—in any obvious sense; e.g. the cat climbing into the flowerpot or Stevens' DISILLUSIONMENT OF TEN O'CLOCK. Or MIDSUMMER NIGHT'S DREAM. What is the point of sticking a pin into a pin?

RC's PIECES—which I dont know—sounds like a reduction of LZ's TO MY VALENTINES in the collection you have. These pieces are not earth-shattering, etc., nor are they meant to be—but they

'Book of poems by Doyle (Victoria: Soft Press, 1970).

could and would be revolutionary if they came out of England or Canada or NZ. I think RC is being playful and if you hear the poem, you would realize it more clearly.

I've never yet seen a poem that wasnt 'literary'—but my own effort is bent on making poetry so transparent that the listener/speaker has experienced the poem before he KNOWS it. In a sense.

RC's work is highly personal; he makes no bones about that. BUT also he wants to bring that privacy of feeling out into the open to see what the feeling means, to see what trueness it has for others. When, at least, he is working well. RD's Vietnam deals, what I've seen, dont come off for me. but it is unlikely that any poetry of that war— except possibly by a Vietnamese—will hold fire beyond some immediate propaganda value. R[obert] D[uncan], of course, likes a certain slackness, so as not to inhibit the flow of his 'meditations'. He's a very literary guy and most literate. But a most stimulating soul.

Imagine yourself trying to make a living thru your poetry. You have to go out and present it to others and hope that they will be moved enough, satisfied enough, to want to insure your survival. Or dont imagine it; try it. (It has been done, in our time, and perhaps it is more vital in our time than ever before that it be done so.)

I want to make you feel more acutely, the risk required—which is NOT an intellectual matter. As for 'understanding', you'll come to it when the time comes. Patience. If saying so ever helps.

My best & come again,

Cid –

LETTER 4

Utano
23rd July 1967

Dear Charles,

LZ these days can be very cranky. A polite and sensible note, however, would be ok. But dont mention my name—for he can be rough on me for pushing others onto him. The thing is simply that the years have brought him aches, as to most, and he has never sought attention. (Still, quietly, he wont be hurt by thoughtfulness.)

The "point" finally, of course, is not what any of these people are doing—but what you are doing.[2] No matter how bad other people's work is, it doesn't improve one's own one jot by H— making comparisons. There is enough you can find that IS poetry and it is against that you may measure, if you must.

Your job is not to satisfy editors, but to provide them the goods—so that they are suddenly editors for the first time.

Basil Bunting is teaching at U of C Santa Barbara for another year. It might be worth leaving New Haven, if you could swing it, and go out there to be within talking range for a year. I dont know him personally, but we have had letters and his poetry alone is enough. He's solid. And apparently more personally accessible than LZ. (FULCRUM has reissued all his work.[3] He'll also, I hear, be having something in the August issue of POETRY.)

Yours always

Cid –

[2] This comment follows a discussion of a variety of critics and poets including M.L. Rosenthal.

[3] Press and magazine run by poet Stuart Montgomery. At Doyle's instigation, prompted by Peter Quartermain of UBC, the English poet Basil Bunting was visiting professor at the University of Victoria for the academic year of 1971-1972, a not altogether happy experience for Bunting or the university.

LETTER 5

Utano
12th August 1967

Dear Charles,

your effort to get at things is too genuine of impulse and gentle in pitch ever to be unwarranted—for me.

Please dont mistake things I say. It is as likely for me to be 'off' as anyone else—and you should take it all with a grain of salt, as perhaps you do. The hope, as I'm sure I've said already, is that it proves reasonably stimulating, all the chatter, and a little illuminating—even if only accidentally.

Economy is not parsimony. What LZ, for me, brings decisively home, reinforces in my own sense of poetry, is the utter weight and integrity of what one is saying, to the point of it singin. Or why CLEVERNESS is weak. But this is not the same as playfulness or wit. The poem should not be reporting back to the writer, but on to the reader-listener-sayer: the re-maker. Very few poems are of this order, unfortunately. As for [Zukofsky's] THE, I'm not clear why you are having difficulties—the thematics of the opening are rather clearly developed as the various contexts are brought together, mother and son, relations, via key myths of our Western world ('out of olde bokes, in good feith'). Z is almost always careful to cue the reader to what he is up to—though his mind moves unexpectedly (you can never guess what the next phrase will be in any poem—even when the structure is very marked) and with unusual agility. 'A-18' should be in the August POETRY: I wont be seeing it for another month or so.) Naturally we can differ in our sense of what is or is not 'labored'. I never find LZ so—though I have often felt unusual labor involved and invoked. His inventiveness and ability to make language yield its maximum are astonishing. He couldnt have occured, it is tru, without EP and WCW—but no one has drawn more out of them and gone so far beyond. He doesnt negate them, of course, but rather reaffirms their accomplishments. And I feel, perhaps mistakenly, that these three

ARE the main line—at least for the USA—and possibly for English poetry everywhere. D[enise] L[evertov] has picked up from WCW, not LZ. Her latest book is weaker for me, tho there are a few nice poems in it. THE JACOB'S LADDER is perhaps her best book to-date. [Bunting's] BRIGGFLATTS is a lovely poem—one of the distinct pleasures I've had in the past few years of poetry.

Love always

Cid–

LETTER 6

Utano
29th August 1967

Dear Charles,

#7 [of the current series of *ORIGIN*] is out and on its way: a good issue[4] dont confuse my poetry with any dogmatics. Unfortunately many do. There are an infinite number of approaches and all valid. Stevens' gaudiness doesnt attract me at all, but his imaginative quickness and the quiet fulness of his mind and language. The delight. Recently received LZ's PREPOSITIONS (volume of essays done by Rapp & Carroll, London): a marvellous collection for anyone who makes poetry or is interested in the making. His comments on WCW, EP, Stevens et al are unusually sharp and cogent. (Agreement is never at issue.)

Tomlinson I've never met, but his work is too intellectually run. The English seem to fear seeming unsophisticated as the worst of all possible things and, as a result, the language never moves except on rails.

Your quote on a NZ poet[5] presses the Whitman allusion too heavy and adds verbiage to– –that—what might better have been:

Luckier
perhaps. Different.
Fall
and the light-boned birds
go
but not as far.

4 Of **Origin**, Series 3.

5 A.R.D. Fairburn.

The American scene is a sick one and must worsen. Next year will tell much, being an election year; i.e., how far the people there are capable of going.

Roethke had moments of openness, but mainly weak and self-pitying to an inordinate degree. Lowell is too neat usually and equally involuted. Dugan is horrible. Dickey a joke. Wordmongers.

Enjoy whatever you can and SEE, HEAR, TASTE, FEEL. But you'll find yourself most extended by the line I've indicated.

Love always

Cid–

LETTER 7

Utano
18th September 1967

Dear Charles,

.... RC's new book (WORDS) recently arrived. His technics are close to my own, but that's about as far as it goes. The self-preoccupation depresses me—as well as himself. It is too small a world—and honesty, if that's what it is, means not enough in that scope.

'A' modulates between a prose swing and an almost too tight poetry. Extraordinary. I havent seen 18 yet, but it is being sent. Z seems more intellectual than he, in fact, is. For me Lorine is the best female buy in US poetry since Marianne Moore—and warmer. Her wit, her genuineness, her voice, her perceptions, her language, all are fine. And the care always comes through into music.

[Andre] DuBouchet is symptomatic of the best in European poetry now: it is 'dry' wine—but if you begin to get into his way of seeing and grasping, there is penetration and possibility. But it is not generally congenial to natives of English. (The abstractness of French is more substantive than the same in English—so that the quality—and there is much music—is hard to bring across.)

[William] Bronk is special: out of Stevens mostly but into something that comes nearer Beckett. For me 'mortality' IS the life in life. Language tastes of it.

Unfortunately ORIGIN is receiving very little support and a main portion of that little threatens to be pulled out from under me by next year. Tough sledding. 50 individual subscribers, you'll admit, isnt much. ($10 is only the same as POETRY and I'm willing to compare values, if that's ever at issue. Not with you, or course.)

I want to shout
Goodbye!
No.
No

man can leave
what he has been through.

I'd leave it at that. The rest is melodrammer. EP's Say what you have
to say and stop—remains sound advice. (I wish he followed it himself.) HAPPENINGS seems (sic) like something from the 20s. Dated
and empty, but activity for those involved; it keeps them out of mis-
chief. But nothing for me that holds fire. WCW's phrase is ok, but it
could be clearer—what constitutes "perception". Luckily we have his
poems. My own poems have sometimes seemed so obvious that people wonder—like my mother—if they are poems at all. that a poem
can be clear to transparency seems to have gotten lost in the shuffle of
ambiguities, etc. But more to center, for me, is that poetry is the
human hearth, as all art is—i.e., when an individual has realized experience at depth in such a way that it can be shared for as long as man.

My love to Bob C — if you meet him — to yourselves — always —

Cid

LETTER 8

Utano
16 October 1967

Dear Charles,

glad that the meeting with RC went well—but everyone I know who has met him (casually) has enjoyed the experience and he is always cordial to young writers. And encouraging.

I have a brief review of WORDS to appear in ELIZABETH (small mag out of NY) sometime next year. His own feeling about it— from your account—tallies well enough with my own. He has always achieved fine poems in the face of the impossibly constricting—but it is often wearing to read him at length: too much intensity going. And his wit is no relief. But that's the way he is and it is something that technique alone wont solve. Technically, in fact, he is remarkable. But he has concerns that very much overlay with my own: it is in content we differ radically—our sense of life itself. But the years may bring us closer again....

Logan I've never met, but have corresponded with: his work is a weak offshoot of Lowell and has not much attracted me—tho he's probably a decent sort of guy. Bly I cant bear as a human being and his poetry leaves me unconvinced. Your sense of them sounds accurate.

Take whatever criticism I offer for what it may be worth. It is only too clear our sense of things differs—even as they should. RC's taste and mine have also reflected sharp differences—though we have often also found major sympathies in common: e.g., Zukofsky. "A"-18 magnificent stuff.

Love always — & to your family

Cid

LETTER 9

Utano
31st October 1967

Dear Charles,

yes, I had thought you were younger than you are. And that, for all I know, may be a high compliment. In fact, however, it mostly tells how your own search overlays with that of others who are younger. There is no time schedule in such matters. My own dream is to make some poetry yet—maybe 20 years hence—that will bear life utterly into the open for others. It is enough for now that I feel the work moving in that "direction'. That is, the dying is clearer all the time. Or why all the clever lines of an Auden, for me, backfire. The poetry must stop saying— Look at me, I'm poetry. Lou Johnson, I know, is a contemporary of mine. I always hoped he would send me something I might like, but I'm afraid he never succeeded. (No doubt, he feels the same of my own work, though I'm not sure he has ever seen much of it or would want to.)

LZ writes that 'A' 13-21 will be published by J Cape next year and that will pull everything together. He is into "A"-22 now and probably will complete the book in the next 3-5 years.

I wouldnt be offended to wear someone else's "drawers," if I lacked for my own. But CO, of course, requires a special size and wouldnt want to be cramped where it hurts.[6]

LZ is a quiet soul. He is not well enough to want much company—but he does respond to courtesy and thoughtfulness. If you are truly interested in his work, etc., that in itself is warrant. But you should phone first. (Dont say that I pushed, however, though my name may be freely used otherwise—if it comes to that.)

---

[6]The reference to "drawers" in paragraph 3 above alludes to an exchange of letters between Doyle and Charles Olson. Doyle found an unattributed poem in the SUNY Buffalo Poetry Collection. He wrote to Olson to ask if it was his. Olson replied that he felt as if he had been accused of wearing someone else's dirty underwear! The poem proved to be by Walter Lowenfels.

E[dward] Thomas I've read—first in connection with Frost, many years ago. I like his work well enough and almost purchased his collected poems a year or two ago—but nothing I need to have "around". I like the clean clear language he generally stays with, of course. But dont imagine that I am incapable of enjoying the rhetorical affluence of a Stevens or a Dylan Thomas or Hart Crane. Ted Enslin is likely in NYC now; Clayton Eshleman would know.

Sam Morse is an old friend; a very New England sort. Flossie Williams has written me of possibly coming over here herself and please do encourage her, if her health permits. We'd love to have her as our guest (if she is coming alone). In any case, to see her and have time with her. A lovely person. Noel Stock I only know has written a book on EP. I dont value my comments highly; whatever use they are, fine. Up to you. And I hope the voice is as different from my own as possible.

Keep me on.

Love always — to you and yours—

Cid

LETTER 10

Utano
19th November 1967

Dear Charles,

am sorry that LZ responded so.[7] But you see now that my anxiety about how to write him was not exaggerated. He has been rather harsh lately with a number of younger people. and tho I can sense that he is merely trying to protect his energies, I wish he had the ability to deal less sharply with many. Perhaps, he was bugged by the double-take—which was unfortunate—as if you had overdone the issue by pressing it thru Flossie. (He is extremely touchy in such matters and I have felt the backlash on more than one occasion when I have had only indirect relation and ALWAYS with the kindest intentions—as he well knows. And I am closer to him, perhaps, than anyone else of my generation.) It is, in its own way, the main weakness in his work too: an unwillingness to sense that he isnt always communicating. A distance is intervening. Homer KNEW his audience and we still feel his presence yet. But in the face of ALL there is, and it is SO much, ok. And he is, in person, a gentle soul — embittered by undeserved neglect, but one who has also cultivated that neglect. (I know enough of what it feels like to appreciate it fully.)

Holly [Stevens], I'm sure, is quite different and should be a satisfaction. Floss is a sweetheart, though she can be pretty sassy. Her energy and clearmindedness are astonishing

P[aul] B[lackburn]'s work is intelligent and he has a good ear—but it is a mimic's ear unfortunately. And I miss an authentic voice. What he is SAYING has never cut deep with me. And lately it seems to me bookish—even, or especially, when he takes to the vernacular. It isnt HIS language: he simply is attracted by it—understandably

---

7 Doyle had written to Zukofsky, but had been rebuffed, despite the fact that Florence Williams had also written Z on Doyle's behalf. Doyle wished to talk with him about William Carlos Williams, but in Zukofsky's view this amounted to an attempt to exploit him.

enough. What you quote seems pretty straight quotation. No more, no less. And precisely the elliptical syntax has drawn him. In American Eng: normally: "up at your house'.

You saw, perhaps, the big chunk of RD's DAY BOOK (HD) in ORIGIN's 2nd series. That was the first of the book to appear and it reflects my own choices from the whole—which I had in ms. RD is bright. (I have the Jung book here—but frankly I find him tedious and not penetrating. Levi-Strauss is much more "on the track' these days. His MYTHOLOGIQUES will be a landmark for further penetrations. But these people are still slow—for me.) Olson has some sense of it, but twists and diddles in his own plethoric consciousness.

#8 will be out in another week or so. The editor of MEANJIN[8] is — suddenly — in contact with me.

Do you know anything about him (Christensen)?–

Love always,

Cid

---

[8] An Australian quarterly.

LETTER 11

Utano
13th December 1967

Dear Mike,

Dont know the PB poems you refer to. Paul has a good ear, but is mostly mockingbird at best. May Swenson I met before she had become "known" and she had me going over her work in detail. But nothing I ever cottoned to. And tho she has become cleverer and craftier, it is work that leaves me cold. A nice enough person, as I recall.

Auden is THE professional poet; i.e., it is a biznis with him. After reading his DYER'S HAND I've just abt had enough. The skill is undeniable and the intelligence—but these things mean nothing to me without the balls. To be vulgar.

Baxter's stuff I've seen and Curnow I know personally (from America—when Thomas was circulating). I've seen a good deal of AC's work and nothing that has ever struck me.

I wish you could see your way NOT to publish or TRY to publish work that you yourself feel less than firm about. I fear that you will find publication too easy.

I still remain the most prolific poet of our time. Enough work for 10 books on hand. But it is simply a constant with me: I write 365 days of each year: it is not WORK for me but delight and it is always a way of REALIZING. There are also translations

Love always and best of the holidays to you and family,

Cid

LETTER 12

Utano
14th January 1968

Dear Mike,

.... To give you a sense of poetry that is, no doubt, not usual—
but still— encouraging—a young French poet [Rene Daumal], who
I'll be featuring in ORIGIN this year, completely unknown as yet,
wrote a long poem (over 50pp) and wrote it evidently with great care
over quite a period of time. He waited 4 years to show it to anyone!
(And he had never published, as far as I know, anything before.) Some
of it was finally printed last year in a mag—which I happen to receive.
It impressed me and I made contact. The entire poem has just been
published as a book and it will appear in ORIGIN: it will require nearly a whole issue: as #10. I mention this as an instance of the fact that it
is possible to WAIT until one has something solid to show. And at a
time when so much junk is being peddled, it almost becomes a NEED
to take one's time. I've just recently myself made versions of poems
begun over a decade ago that begin to satisfy me, poems that have
gone thru countless transformations. (And even poems of a few lines
or a few words—of mine—often represent years of consideration and
reconsideration. that they dont SOUND like it is a satisfaction. But it
is also why imitators fail.) I hope Wesleyan turns you down—but fear
they wont. It isnt that your work isnt as good as much else that they
print, if not all, but THAT isnt any criterion, or shouldnt be. And you
have nothing to PROVE. You exist and you are working: you know it
and those who care know it. The quieter you operate, the more
patience you have with letting you voice, your deeper soundings,
emerge—the truer will be the poetry. It will BE poetry, in short.
I have no faith that anything I say can be of much use—but it
may, since it is accurate to my own being, provide some adequate fric-
tion.
Recently NOTHING I read satisfies me, in poetry: everything
seems pretty or clever or vomit (*vide* Eshleman's WALKS, etc). And

"sincerity" is a red herring. When I read Homer or Shakespeare the notion of sincerity never has time to enter. There is only the feeling of an entire life thrown into the breach (death). And that's all that we have to face the emptiness with and thru: more of the same, but EMBODIED. I.e., what to touch others with: to sound each emptiness....

Take care & love always,

Cid

LETTER 13

Utano
8th February 1968

Dear Mike,

BOTTOM[9] is full of lovely things. But like LZ you WONT enjoy the work unless you read it ALOUD and SAVOR each word. On the other hand your sense of it is understandable enough; it just dont "enter", that's all. Of course, it does relate to 'A'. All the man's work is of a piece.

Holly Stevens also mentioned Sister Bernadetta (?) recently.[10] Her name has been familiar for some time—but I dont recall any of her words—just the overlay of interests. Blackburn is in Europe now, I believe. Wright I dont know. His poetry neither attracts me nor offends me. Bly, unfortunately, I once met and that has tended to color my reading of his work, perhaps unfairly, negatively.

Had a warm account by a young poet of LZ's recent reading at the Guggenheim. (LZ himself had written of it—but only indicated the emotional strain of the event—always the case with him, as with most of us.) I'm sorry not to be able to attend such occasions—but enough that 'A' continues—and the recent sections have been brilliant and beautiful. Denny Levertov has written some nice poems. Yes, she has acquired a voice, but she can still play it false.

Love to you & your gang always,

Cid –

---

[9] Book by Louis Zukofsky.

[10] Sister M. Bernetta Quinn, at that time known as author of a critical work, **The Metamorphic Tradition in Modern Poetry.**

LETTER 14

Utano
15th March 1968

Dear Mike,

let's see. Anyhow, first—glad that you've cleared the next step. And it will put you near a young Canadian poet that I've known for some time (since he was 17!) who has been hung on drugs for several years now, but underneath is a good sort and with fair promise—if he can get a hold of himself and throw his heart into the world more. Name of Victor Coleman.[11] Once you're in them parts you'll likely get wind of him. (Never went to college, but bright.)

[Robin] Blaser is the person you missed, unfortunately, at Simon Fraser and probably the one person worth meeting: a person I like very much. His poetry isnt quite strong enough for me, but intelligent and thoughtful and a sweet guy. He was very close to Jack Spicer and John Wieners. (These people come out of Boston, my hometown, so that connections occur subterraneously.) Anyhow, no reason you cant contact these people.

You come with a broader spectrum than most and can afford to be open to everything, as you should be. No sense making people close off in advance.

Len Cohen I dont know personally, but know his work and reputation. And we have many friends in common. Not really attractive to me. The rhetorical school. But in freewheeling Layton fashion, a little updated. Kearns I know, as it were, from his infancy—with the TISH group in Vancouver. Not bad. But the Canadians run thin....

Merwin I dont like as a poet. Most unconvincing man: every book a new style, trying to stay fashionable; it wont work. For all his

---

[11] Doyle contacted Coleman, who later, as editor of Coach House Press, Toronto, published one issue of **Tuatara** magazine (no. 2) and Doyle's sequence of poems, **Earth Meditations** (Toronto: Coach House Press, 1971).

craftiness. Next week JDickey in town for a couple of days and I've been asked to care for him. I can be decent towards him—regardless that his work is off for me. But it may even be salutary for me to get a clearer sense of such "poets".

Love Always——

Cid–

LETTER 15

Utano
14th April 1968

Dear Mike,

I'm sure the WCW industry is immense and will grow more so. But it wont alter the quality or character of his work and/or life one iota—so it carries little or no meaning for me. I suppose there will be eventually more "original" material published (many more letters, for example, that postdate the previous collection that tell much about his influence with my generation especially). someone named Weaver in England wrote me recently and mentioned he was doing a WCW book. So it goes....

RD is a bright guy and, I feel, capable of writing elegant poetry—and there are plenty of solid instances in, say, THE OPENING OF THE FIELD (I havent seen more than bits of more recent items). But he tends towards the cultist. He is extremely "literary" in the literal sense: he lives and breathes books. (I cant—though I have my devotions too.) "Posturing"? Perhaps, but stylish.

Coleman is keeping in touch now and sounds like he may rise out of himself yet. Spicer is interesting usually—but it doesnt go far enough. Blaser is nicer as a person. Wieners has produced some touching poems—but sadly has been overpraised to his own detriment.

Dickey was pleasant enough personally—but a very sad guy. And his work (he gave me a copy of the new pb.) just DONT make it for me: too roily and overblown. But he has a core of frightened genuineness that meeting him clarified. We had quite a bit of time alone to gab and drink together. And he does LIKE to talk. Often just to himself....

Love & best on the new moves,

Cid

LETTER 16

Utano
15th June 1968

Dear Mike,

As with Canada, Australia, etc., the surprising thing, in the arts—i.e., in the world of human imagination, is that ANYTHING occurs. ONE poet is extraordinary. One painter. Etc. For you must realize how rare such a person is ANYWHERE. No doubt, it is more UNLIKELY there than where the general level of achievement has been higher over quite a period of time and the audience is geared to higher performance, etc. The imagination has begun to permeate society—unconsciously.

I'm airing you separately a batch of the education MEMOes.[12] Just put them where they will be read. Older people are likely to be completely indifferent to it; it will seem too much SF to them and unrelated to their immediacy. But it touches on issues that are international, though it cannot explore any one sector of the vision at any depth naturally. I do mean to follow it up—but after I've done considerably more reading in the pertinent literature (which has been accumulating, I discover, over the past decade) and mulling of responses, etc. I want to get down to basic issues and let the technologists, etc., take it from there. But I have yet to read ANYONE on the subject of education (thru all of man's history) or HEAR anyone speak of education with any sense of what it is all about. It is not really surprising, of course, bumbles and fumbles in the very area of existence that provides the basis of all that is "off" in human society. As it is, today the issues are being brought home as never before—and the situation promises to get considerably graver yet. Another year and I expect the international student revolution to be well under weigh. Even to get anyone in the world of education to THINK ABOUT these

---

[12] Corman had recently written a pamphlet on education, which he circulated privately.

issues is difficult. It undermines their personal morale and they feel utterly impotent. One friend here, and quite bright, says frankly he wont discuss the issues with me (he is a professional teacher in Toronto area and will be the rest of his life) because he knows it is futile! I've done a fair amount of teaching and—informally—an immense amount. And I have evolved techniques radically different from any in use now—and especially vital, I feel, in the presentation of literature and language. But it really opens into every sphere of human thought and action.

The educators everywhere, and teachers, are a pretty hopeless lot to deal with....

Love to you both,

Cid and Shizumi

LETTER 17

Utano
29th June 1968

Dear Mike,

good letter and all the more since so few have responded to the memo at all. (#10, en passant, will be with you shortly too.)

Everything you say in apparent extension of what I have written accords with my own feeling. Technology, like books, is an instrument. At the rate things are going now, however, technology is doing the dictating, largely because educators dont know how to cope with it, or even know what they are doing—without it. I.e., no one has really faced what education is all about. (The Framingham school—I have nephews and nieces in that town, as well as other friends—may or may not be any good. What you quote as objectives ok, but it doesnt mean that the actuals will connect at any depth, and they dont get at the core of the experience.) I've been reading all the classic material on the subject I can find, but nothing impresses me and most of it horrifies me.

Schools are not necessary at all. And of course the use of technology I have in mind is precisely that which would use it as an adjunct to that more vital relation of being elicited WITHIN the actual community, whatever it might be. The school is always an artificial community within a given community and is false even within its own limits. For each "subject" is another artificial community. And relation of teacher and student rarely includes any sense of responsibility.

The individual teacher CAN make a tremendous difference, but that usually occurs only at the highest levels, or in most isolate instances (a small country school, where teacher IS a community). Read the Penguin (PELICAN SPECIAL) RISING HILL by Leila Berg—recently out. this fellow Duane is a most unusual soul—sounds fictional. And myself I never had any teacher, AS such, who taught me anything. Except, of course, "the system".

My thesis is that ALL children, including those with congenital defects, etc., the so-called "retarded" ones, are geniuses; i.e., that they have immense capacities of imagination and the power to project realization. But these endowments are effectively crushed in virtually all within a few years of schooling, if not earlier at home. (Reading Rousseau's CONFESSIONS, in French, now; he writes beautifully; and it bears me out handsomely.)

The set-up that you project is only feasible in such a technological array as I suggest. The situation we face is irreversible; we have to deal with it. And I do feel that we, precisely the poets, must. Those of us who still do have a residue of imagination must see that it isnt violated indefinitely.

And of course you are quite right in mentioning the scarcity of imagination. Not peculiar to NZ.

I'm writing, it will take much of the summer I think, a book on education—thoroughly anecdotal and specific in character—which will run about 250pp. (I dont concern myself with publishing of it; it will be too radical for most, if not all, and I may be forced to do it myself.)

But generalities wont carry enough weight without a clear sense of the daily practice involved behind them. (My own "teaching" experiences are unusual and extensive—at all levels—with children and adults. And on three continents.)

You say teacher was most vital in your own experience. Is that accurate? Wasnt parent more vital? Wasnt a fellow-student or two just as vital? I dont know—but no teacher touched me as such in the formal situation—though two special events in my early career were of import. And they will enter my book. If you can tell me of a key educational experience in your own life, I'd be grateful (in some detail)— either positive or negative. And check with your wife too.

Love from us both to all of you,

Cid and Shizumi –

LETTER 18

Utano
8th July 1968

Dear Mike,

congratulations on not making out with Wesleyan. Your being known in NZ is ok; that's very local. But on the larger scene I feel you should have much stronger work to show—and there is absolutely NO RUSH. When the poems are there, you'll know; and if not, not.

Just had a letter today from the lady who wrote the Pelican RISING HILL book—which is worth looking at. It reads rapidly. She tells me that the book was kept from appearing 2 years ago, by lawyers, for fear the issue was too hot then. No doubt. But ironically she quotes a personal letter from this fellow Holt who is the target of the book I am now writing! Connections are sometimes extraordinary. Actually Holt is only the specific and my attack is on the lack of imagination in education and the need of a clearer sense of what it is all about. (Frankly, reading all the experts recently, I cannot find ANYTHING that even remotely suggests a sense of what it is all about, as if no one had ever really thought about it. Yet, in conversation, many friends speak well on the matter. And I see that there is a superficial agreement often that breaks down on examination and especially when actual practise is discussed.)

Muggy hot here. Reading Rousseau's CONFESSIONS (in French) and find much pleasure in his excellent prose. He sounds fresher than the "moderns": e.g., Marguerite Duras or Albert Camus—stylistically, if not in content. (But their content is often their style or stylishness.) They write so laboriously.

Also the Opies' attractive book on CHILDREN'S LORE & LANGUAGE. Amazing that at least 1/3rd of the material they collect was familiar to me in my childhood. We all know more poetry than we realize.

Love to you & family always,

Cid & Shizumi –

LETTER 19

Utano
27th July 1968

Dear Mike,

your booklet in and much thanks.[13]
You begin to try to use language relaxedly, but the whole thing
strikes me as a negative venture — not unlike, say, much of NY paint-
ing during and after the war — immediately — trying to "break away"
from the "line", but only implying it more.
Still — ok.
At last — it suggests you are hearing others: Creeley, Duncan,
LZ, Kelly, etc. What I miss is YOU.
The "news" enclosed is too talky and unoriginal. I dont feel that
it cost you anything — certainly nothing that is central.
And the movement is, for all the brevity, dull. It is readable
enough, to be sure, but without any music, any deeper sounding. And
so very literary.
The desire to break loose is there, but not the event of it. It aint
coming off. Which doesnt mean to stop. Even if you feel discouraged.
Dont TALK so much — but let your life sing.
Looked quickly at the Penguin NEW AUSTRALIAN WRITING
and none of the poetry seems worth a damn to me. My Aussie friend
here — tho he has quite a ways to go yet has more going than any of
that. I wish he were as rich a human being as he is a keen mind.
Dont imagine that I'm incapable of writing a warm enthusiastic letter about anyone's poetry. Nothing excites me more — but it is
a rare event.

---

[13] **Earth Meditations: 2**, privately printed in Auckland in 1968. This sequence
recently appeared in Big Smoke: New Zealand Poems 1960-1975 (Auckland University Press, 2000). One of that book's editors wrote to Doyle: "a very influential piece,
then and in retrospect". —Alan Brunton to MD, e-mail, 26 July 2000.

Only lines in your piece I trust — and they are quite modest:

"treading woodland's mulching leaves...
...sat
at a cook-out bench by Branch brook
thumbing duncan's ROOTS & BRANCHES."

Love always,
Cid –

LETTER 20

Utano
10th August 1968

Dear Mike,

No debate abt your poem: no one can know better than yourself its merits and demerits and uses. Take anything I say as encouragement.

Kelly's qualities I think you will understand better if you spend
a few hours in conversation with him. I'd like to see some samples of
[Gordon] Challis's versions of Vallejo (from the POEMAS
HUMANOS, of course) to compare with C[layton] E[shleman]'s.
Clayton gets Vallejo's energy ok, but he misses the man's fineness —
taking rawness for crudity. And often CE simply doesnt understand
his original. (My Spanish is thin, but I know poetry too well to muff
things that he does.)

Layton is so much a part of an "old" Canadian scene. Yes, he
has good moments—the best at the time I was publishing him, in fact,
a dozen years or more ago. But he has never matured and his voice is
"dominion". Margaret Avison writes with far more intelligence and
grace. But Canada has not yet had a deep and genuine voice in literature. It may come, however.

Love always — to all,

Cid and Shizumi

Letter 21

Utano
15th November 1968

dear Mike,

A strange thing I suddenly realized in glancing over old letters: that Marianne Moore had grave doubts as to what I was printing in the 1st series of ORIGIN, whereas Stevens was remarkably enthusiastic throughout. That 1st series is being reprinted now in NYC by the KRAUS people and that pleases me, for the stuff has been so long unavailable and now it bids fair to be as "around' as long as people want it. And since I edit with a longterm sense of bearing, issues of ORIGIN at any point remain "alive' — or so I feel. #13 will go to the printers in 3 weeks or so. It will be almost unreadable for most and there will be little space to evade the poetry involved — for it takes up almost the entire space. A young French poet virtually unknown even in Paris: the issue is a version of his entire work to-date. The vein is unlike anything in English, as yet, but for me exciting.[14]

Yours — always,

Cid –

---

[14] Rene Daumal

LETTER 22

Utano
22 December 1968

Dear Mike,

You should contact Daphne Marlatt in Vancouver. She's involved in teaching too and is likely to be sympathetic and helpful. And Doug Woolf also. (He's mostly a migrant worker, so he lives in and out of a car — but a fine person and a gifted writer.)

Mike Weaver in England must have his book on B[lack]M[ountain] about ready for printing. And Cape-Goliard is bringing out a selection of Olson's letters to me, edited by a former student of his at Buffalo, this spring, to be called THE ORIGIN LETTERS, mostly — I understand — in relation to editing a little mag, etc. I cant recall that CO had so much to say on the subject that meant anything to me. But he was, initially, interested. His most revealing letter, however, I didnt sell to Texas and still have: a small part of it will appear in ELIZABETH in the coming year. (You should, by the way try some of your work with Jim Weil (of LIZ), 103 Van Etten Blvd., New Rochelle, NY 10804. He's quite a decent soul (studied at Oxford and is almost exactly your age and has several children) and, though imitative (mostly of my work and Ted Enslin's), not a bad poet.

Love & best of years to

you & yours,

Cid & Shizumi–

LETTER 23

953 Hampshire Rd
Victoria, B.C.
Jan. 18, 1969

Dear Cid:

I enjoyed your letter. When it came we were virtually snowed in and taking an enforced, very valuable and welcome "quiet period". The snow continues, an unusual thing for here, but circumstances I like very much.

Recently I read *Frames* (now published as a volume) and, alas, I do not greatly care for it. This is partly because I don't care for "The Snow Queen", but I find something puzzling about Daphne Marlatt's writing. It very often seems to me banal, and perhaps this is a result of avoiding being "literary", but the whole conception of **Frames** is literary.

I found the chance, too, to read nos.11 and 12. The best in no. 11 are your own small things and that little Niedecker (With her things there's always a sense of immediate contact). Denis Goacher makes me somewhat uneasy, with his "brilliant aeroplanes", "glittering moment", "neat like dolls houses" and "even the nuns stopped praying". I sometimes wonder if I am missing a proper sense of the value of the commonplace, but surely that's not it? Goacher does have his moments of clarity, but the above examples make one wonder how fortuitous they are.

In contrast I respond to Faust's poem in no. 12. Seems to me he has an ear more finely attuned than Goacher, and a surer sense of what may be simple and fresh. Glad to have the Chuang-Tzu, which I shall read and savour over a period.

Much interested to hear about the Cape-Goliard publication of Olson letters. Have been thinking about CO, rereading, finding again the exciting concreteness of *Mayan Letters*. (Curious how "letters" and "interviews" have, in the 'sixties, taken on full status as lit'ry works. The appetite for "facts" again?): O's proposition about SPACE seems to me important, if not entirely clear. He seems to follow Whitehead (as WCW did with his interpenetration, I imagine) in claiming that man relates to world as part of a single field of energy. How then — SPACE? In such circs. the notion of Space itself wd seem too rigid; but O is correct in putting his finger on the central weakness in **Paterson** — Bill Williams' over-regard for history. Yet, of course, **Paterson** is both a place (space) and has a history.

O's mind seems much more vigorous and in contact than Creeley's (RC apparently is back in New Mexico for a year) and much more concrete than Robt Duncan's (I really am irritated by much of RD's latest book). It cd be said that RC's work is more of a coherency, but Olson is the one who really counts there.

Do you have the specific details of Mike Weaver's Black Mountain project? Where it is to be published, etc? I had a very brief look at some of the material when W was at Yale, and of course I would like to have the stuff as soon as may be. I knew W slightly at New Haven (where he was working on a background-autobiographical book on WCW). We agreed to keep in touch, but we are not altogether of a type and there has been nothing to communicate so far. On that line, a chap I know at Buffalo (Mazzaro) is just editing a book of essays on Modern American Poetry and plans to follow it with another centred on Black Mountain. There's every likelihood that I shall be asked to contribute. (I heard about this only two days ago). It occurs to me as I write now that there's no reason why I should not contribute something on the part played in the "movement" (I realize it isn't really, or simply, that) by yourself and **Origin**. I know that you rightfully distrust critics (as I do myself when it comes to my own work!) but if there are going to be any, always the poets themselves bring most imagination to the task. What do you think?

Love to Shizumi and yourself,

Mike –

LETTER 24

Utano
23rd January 1969

dear Mike,

yes — if anything is to be written about ORIGIN and my part in the so-called B[lack] M[ountain College] "scene' — I'd prefer someone like yourself to do it. At any rate, in such matters I have a penchant for accuracy and my memory is pretty reliable and where it fails me, I am frank in admitting — and perhaps could suggest "checkpoints" anyhow. And if you arent called upon to contribute to that deal, dont feel that I'm in any way disturbed. As I think you know, publicity is something I have gone out of my way to avoid and have lost a few "friends" in the process and bid fair to continue to add to the list. My concern is with the work and I would wish the accent to be kept there and not on balance-sheets. Or credits. (Despite that this obviously cuts out a lot of personal credit.)

I'm enclosing a piece — actually just a letter — I wrote at the suggestion of Dean Keller, a librarian and the editor of THE SERIF [Vol. V #1, March 1968] at K[ent]S[tate]U[niversity] — which may be of use to you and I've added some marginalia that offer more details. Everything here is accurate and there are no false emphases, etc.

You'll have questions, if you get involved, and I'll help you in what ways I can — and as long as they dont require too much of my energies — since I'm uptomyneck in labors now and labors that seem to me far more vital.

You touch upon some of the weaknesses of FRAMES, but you seem not see the strengths of it and that is a pity. But your very criticism of it suggests that you might very well be of service to Daphne. [Anthony]Hecht is a barrel of shit, as they say. The [Howard] Nemerov-[Howard]Moss-[Louis] Simpson gang. All very bright and witty and who-could-care-less. Of these people Dick Wilbur remains more attractive to me, because less pretentious and more genuine. Lowell has some grace and there is a streak of basic sincerity in him that holds fire — for all the folderol. But these people all seem to me backwater at best.

You spend most of your time, it seems, looking for weaknesses: everyone has them. But find the graces. Rare enough, to be sure — but that's where the light belongs — or so I feel.

Yes, CO follows Whitehead. Where we part company. The large constructs invariably miss the home points. And his criticism of PATERSON may be sound, but seems to me largely irrelevant to what Bill actually does. Still — CO's work — the MAXIMUS poems and indeed all his work that he has himself retained in bookform and a bit more — has strength and bite to it. And warrants far more attention than it gets. I weary of so-called critics who still get away with the garbage of evading CO and LZ by calling them Poundlings. CO is often apparently concrete, but he often misses the obvious in his leaps for the constellation. And his Mayan letters dismay me even yet by the simple lack of human feeling as he intellectually masturbates and keeps himself so going. (Not irrelevant, sadly, that his breakup with Con, his 1st wife, who was with him there occurred about 2 years later.) For you and for the "objective' soul this may seem beside the point — but for me it remains central. Havent seen RD's recent work.

Love to you and yours always,

Cid

LETTER 25

Utano
31st January 1969

dear Mike,

it may be that you have a role cut out for you at this point as critic.[15] If so, do keep it open. Or, if you dont feel so, drop it altogether. Halfway measures wont do — or so I feel.

Plenty that warrants discussion in WCW. His incredible zeal in behalf of the young — especially in his later 20 years — the last of his life. And even as Floss has said to me: she used to hide letters from him in the last years, knowing he insisted on answering everything. True. My letter in ORIGIN #1 of this series indicates directly how he affected us and marks one of his key meetings (the one with DL). He often got lost in the welter of EP, as have so many others. Fortunately he did have a distinct voice and intelligence of his own and a quite different personality. (Floss is very much like him: I have often felt that if he didnt write his books, she would have done so.)

Best to write about ORIGIN and B[lack]M[ountain] R[eview] separately. Both merit consideration, I think. But in their own terms. A tacit comparison would be better than any overt one. BMR came out of 2 main causes, I believe: 1) Olson's desire for an organ for himself — but without his editing — he provided the needed cash from BMC, and 2) RC and CO wanted to do things that they felt I was not in a position to do. (We had no quarrels in these matters, as I recall. The frictions I had with either — mostly with RC — were of a different order and not major. RC/CO letters of that time wd no doubt clarify their motives amply.) RC also, candidly, in time, admitted he was jealous of ORIGIN — and since he HAD had the mag idea first, it is quite understandable. And I was pleased that BMR began, if only to relieve this silly tension, which I had felt for some time. BMR picked up the Beats first — via BMC and Duncan. I was in

---

[15] Corman is now responding to Doyle's idea that he write a book about Black Mountain College and Origin magazine. This project never came to fruition.

Italy — in the back country — and had lost contact by then — though I had been informed of the Beats — even before TIME broke the word. I think Indiana U has my WCW letter that told me of them — in late 54 or early 55.

In a blurb for [Larry] Eigner's recent FULCRUM PRESS book ANOTHER TIME IN FRAGMENTS RD writes (The 1st clear statement of the matter): (of LE) "he writes in the mode following Pound's PISAN CANTOS and WCW's later poetry that has been labeled the Black Mt school but began earlier in the magazine ORIGIN in the early 1950's.' That is accurate. I can send you, if you do find yourself really involved in it, the English version of an essay I wrote for a Belgian mag BEFORE I went to Europe (in Sept 54) in which I declare our relation to EP & WCW. It was open and the basis of our allegiance — tho my interest, as I said there and elsewhere, was wider, for it included poets like Bronk and Enslin, who have only slight relation to the BMC line. Enslin did gradually fall under WCW's spell — but this was NOT the case as yet — then.

I was never — of course — at BMC — written remembering that both RD & RC were there only very briefly. (One term each.) CO was the center of it. After Yucatan. (He had been there a bit before.) Jonathan Williams is a native of the region as well & quickly became their "publisher/poet'. The story of how Wieners got there relates to me — that I didn't hear about it till long after. So too — the connections with Ed Marshall/Robin Blaser. ORIGIN, in sum, was the first major focal point for the EP-WCW (mainstream — as I call it) descendancy, after the war.

Love always,

Cid –

46

LETTER 26

Utano
7th March 1969

Dear Mike,

CO's work has a strong historical tendency — and more so more recently. And the sense of space is one of the givens of America — as of China or Russia and clear in their literature. But LZ has both history and space operating. PATERSON is obviously intended to dig a ground and let it parse a nation. Any of these theories has something to be said for it — but they often serve to blind one to what IS done. OK for a poet who wants to do something else — or if you are comparing poets or poetries.[16]

The education book just sits here: I've revised a bit of it — but it wont be till the summer probably that I'll feel inclined to go back to it. My mind is elsewhere occupied right now. #14 will be out in a few weeks and I'm thinking of succeeding issues, as well as work of my own.

There seems to be a deepening interest in Olson, etc. And I expect there'll be a growing sequence of books on his work and ideas. He is more of a stimulus force often than a maker of poems — though sometimes he is both. The years seem only to have refined my prejudices.

Yes, Jim had mentioned your work and taking a couple.[17] His mag is broadening at the base and deepening its quality, I feel. We disagree in many particulars, but he is a thoughtful soul and thoroughly reliable.

Our Kusano book turned out a beauty (a few minor typographical errors — invented after my final proofs) and has had very warm initial notice. It should be in America very soon. [?]

Love to you & yours — always,

Cid

[16] Corman is responding to a letter of Doyle's in which he talked about Olson's idea that America is more spatial than historical.
[17] James L. Weil, editor of **Elizabeth** magazine, founder of the Elizabeth Press.

LETTER 27

Utano
17th April 1968

Dear Mike,

A biography of WCW isnt wise until Floss is gone — and I'm not keen to rush it. (I hope to see her when we visit the States next year.) And anyhow his poems tell all that needs to be said of that. And a little bit too much at that. I think PATERSON and the later poems (though the final batch, apart from some good lyrics here and there, are not as powerful) merit your attention — and of course there are landmarks in the earlier works. He is, for me, the prime force in American poetry: creating the clean phrase and open line without resorting to Whitmanesque cymbals. He brings poetry back to the force of speech itself, language as event, and without hoking up a clever rhetoric — such as has crushed British and affiliated writings for a century now, clogged the stream.

I havent a copy of I[n]T[he]A[merican]G[rain] now and can only say that it meant much to me when I read it — for it demonstrated decisively the poetry of history and how the poetic vision can illuminate all — and is perhaps the only human kindling we have. Apart from the poetry and the stories, those essays and the ones in his collected essays, the letters and AUTOBIOGRAPHY, not read his other proseworks — though I one day will. I always turn by choice to poetry first.

Your reason for TUATARA (Marianne Moore has written of the creature, of course) is not ample or deep enough. You can make contact with other poets you admire or respect without resorting to a mag. I am quite pleased to have you try — but cant help offering some advice. Merely to print poets who are being printed elsewhere has no meaning. CATERPILLAR, for example, has no reason for being except its editor's need for attention and for a place he can be sure will publish his own works. Otherwise he has done nothing of note that hadnt already been done and welldone. EL CORNO, say, is a weak mag, but it does have its own character and its place in the scene: no other mag has chosen to usurp it either. Jim W also does things that no one else is really doing now. What might be useful is if you brought a more international English mag into play — drawing from down-under and England as well as America — but letting your own taste be prism. It can only work well, if you work at a high level. And so make CON-NECTIONS for others. To do the mag merely for yourself is self-indulgence on a scale that will only make you unhappy in the end....

....I was not in D[onald] A[llen]'s anthology because I asked NOT to be: I had, in fact, a contract — which I threw away. I have said no to about 15-20 anthologies — but will appear in Carruth's BAN-TAM anthology [**The Voice That is Great Within Us**] end of this year / early next — for it comes at the right time and reports the whole picture with an unexampled generosity (almost all ORIGIN poets are in it — as well as too many others). H[ayden] C[arruth] an independent. NEW DIRECTIONS will finally issue me — new work — a year hence.

The Kusano book (FROGS. AND OTHERS.) should be available now: Grossmans, NY: about $9. Beautiful book. The Eigner book a good one. (Don Hall in his Penguin antho. gives me a little credit too — tho none of these knows me as poet ironically.)

Delighted to hear — whenever

Love always,

Cid–

LETTER 28

June 5, 1969
Victoria, B.C.
759 Helvetia Cres.

Dear Cid:

ORIGIN 14 is a pleasure. Taggart's work especially appeals to me. Slowly now I can really see what it is you look for. Any whiff of literariness has to go. And I agree, in most moods. Where I stop is that lit. in itself is an area of experience. I make some poems that way (even touched by the old measure) and I can't just deny them any validity. I feel that I have not gone (yet at least, who knows?) nearly as far in your direction as would arrive.

.... I would greatly appreciate being able to use some things from HEARTH. For that, though, I must explain that TUATARA will have something of the same "eclecticism' as ELIZABETH. (Sad that JW is stopping it, but with work and some hope of sensitivity I may help fill the gap.) As I foresee it, you will probably need patience with TUATARA, but I hope you shall; as my sense of things moves, the shift does seem to be greatly in your direction, as I recognise it. I.e., I can't totally abandon, say, James Wright, just as I find it very hard to take some of Eshleman's "people' seriously....

We, too, look forward to meeting you both, and love,

Mike

LETTER 29

Utano
9th June 1969

dear Mike,

you scare me a bit when you speak of now knowing what it is I'm looking for. (Some years ago a US poetaster threw 100s of poems at me for ORIGIN and I threw them right back, but he insisted that he would make me an ORIGIN-type poem; he had succeeded everywhere else.) I'm open to ANYTHING, in fact. I have found no other editor, indeed, as open — without being simply blindly sloppy (like POET-RY).

TUATARA is your thing. Let it be so. Eclecticism for me is almost invariably an excuse for laziness of spirit. There is no sense pretending you are a god sitting above the fray either and thus indifferent to differences. You work from within and wherever you are you have to be acute. And you will find, of course, that you cannot print work better than you receive. And if you dont receive material up to your desires? What do you do then? ....

[Henry] Rago's death should only increase POETRY's stance along conservative lines.[18] I gather he was being aggravated by carpings of a too liberal attitude. I suppose I was the only one who thanked him for giving LZ so much space, etc.

Love always,

Cid–

---

[18] Editor of **Poetry**.

LETTER 30

SENDER'S NAME AND ADDRESS — NOM ET ADRESSE DE L'ENVOYEUR

Doyle,
759 Helvetia Cres.
Victoria, BC.
Canada.

NO ENCLOSURE PERMITTED — NE RIEN INSÉRER
· POSTES CANADA POST

June 22, 1969
759 Helvetia Cres.

Dear Cid:

I am delighted with the Ponge, and with your generosity. So much so that I sat down and wrote off to you immediately on receiving the poem, but I disliked my letter and then my father-in-law turned up from foreign parts and all was put aside to entertain him.

More Ponge would be very welcome (& I shall of course send copies to FP.) My feeling of dissatisfaction with my letter came about because I had enclosed with it two of my poems for you to look at, & then lost confidence in them. Also I attempted to explain that, of course, I do not believe I know all the answers & can easily perceive your view of the poem. I hope I've more diffidence than the poetaster you allude to. I felt, for a moment, a sense of your living in the poem, that's all.

Today I've been working all day in the garden, grew tired & picked up a handful of books. I've been asked to review for Alphabet, a bad Britisher (J.S. Cunningham) whose use of the "open" line is like a case of aural elephantiasis, a weak American (Stanley Koehler), a "solid" but finally dull Canadian, & Pierre Jean Jouve, whose Rapp book opens with some prose excerpts, the first being: "...I had two fixed objectives in sight: first, to work out a poetic language that would hold its own entirely as song — not one of the lines I had written fulfilled this requirement; and to find in the poetic act a religious perspective — the only answer to the void of time.

Through these twin objectives my mind encountered an upward movement, a movement of consciousness I propose to call "spiritual". This movement has since remained constant throughout my life & work. I've read nothing of Jouve for fifteen years. These translations (by Keith Bosley) seem somewhat wooden & don't "sing" much. But Jouve is a poet & the other three people are not. This paragraph of his seems to me to suggest a way of looking at experience not unlike your own.

Love to yourself & Shizumi,

Mike

LETTER 31

AIR
MAIL

PAR
AVION

AEROGRAMME

Cid Corman
Fukuoji·Cho 82,
UTANO
UKYO·KU, KYOTO 616
JAPAN

Utano
27th June 1969

dear Mike,

perhaps I push you too hard and bring on the stammers. Excuse me. Sometimes my own clearer sense of movement thrusts into what seems both dogmatic and vague to others — and I'm not much given to explanation. Simply that wherever I am, I've arrived slowly.

I do live through poetry and for me living is poetry — or it is nothing. And (?) it is nothing. Jouve's statement is ok — but only the poetry can give it clarity and resonance. (I've translated Jouve in the past and have had a copy of his poems with me for 15 years.) His mingling of sex and spirituality — an old Christian ploy, lord knows — has occasional striking power — and he has a direct lyrical gift at times that reaches me. Pierre Emmanuel, when I first met him (at Harvard

54

in the early 50s — probably 1950 exactly), put me onto PJJ — who was E's spring-board (by his own admission). (I never met Rago either: only a handful of notes between us: my last one, I'm pleased, was one thanking him for providing an adequate place for LZ.) (I dont see POETRY normally either.) CATERPILLAR has usually something redeeming in it — like Duncan's HD work — but it is mostly roily selfpity and noise. "Dry bones": OK — but do better. Not simple, as you will see. And I hope you are tough; dont compromise.

LZ's "A" 13-21 here now and I've gone thru it all now — mostly a 2nd or 3rd time except for "A"-21 (RUDENS) — which I want to check against Plautus' Latin (which I have). LZ remains astonishing and firstrate.

HORSEBACK

Whinnying of the horse of death!
It yields to the temptation of the black mouth–
Below and intimate and of the plaster gaze–
And of the game of bedcurtains, sexes, legs and arms.–
Bare devouring tree, O mother and earth and death!–
Shadow of long history, bleeding mouth.–
Satisfy and condemn man, this long heart–
Aspiring to die within your gluey hand.

Jouve.

And this piece by Ponge:

"TO DREAM SUBSTANCE"

Probably, any and all — and ourselves — are only immediate dreams of the divine Substance:
The textual products of its prodigious imagination.
And so, in a sense, you could say that nature as a whole, man included, is only a form of writing; but writing of a certain kind; a *non-significative* writing, from the fact that it refers to no system of signification; that it deals with an undefined universe: properly speaking *immense*, without measure.

Whereas the world of words is a finite universe.

But due to its being composed of these very particular and particularly moving objects, the significant and articulate sounds of which we are capable, which serve us *at once* by naming the objects of nature and expressing our feelings,

No doubt it is enough to *name* whatever it may be — in a certain way — to express all of man and, at the same stroke, to glorify substance, an example for writing and providence of the spirit.[19]

(1963) from NOUVEAU RECEUIL, 1967 Gallimard

This text is quite accurate and I follow the man's words to a T. It is interesting to contrast with the Jouve you quote. If you want to use the PJJ, ok: from SUEUR DE SANG, Gallimard, 1935. (I note for the 1st time that it is a 1st edition and numbered.) Evidently it was hard to sell 2500 copies — even by 1954. (It sold at about 60 CENTS in '54 — originally less.) #15 [of ORIGIN]should be out within 5 days or so. A nice issue. Eshleman has 18 more poems by Celan for his WORM to be made this summer.

Love always,

Cid –

---

[19] This poem appeared in **Tuatara No. 1**.

LETTER 32

Victoria
August 1, 1969

Dear Cid:

Have just returned from the East (i.e. New Haven, N.Y. and Buffalo) where all seemed sweltering and frenetic. Saw Norman Pearson at Yale and he was about the only civilised person I met that far east. New Haven itself has changed in eighteen months and feels violent.

At Buffalo I met a young poet, Allen de Loach, whom I found OK. His own poems are not (or not yet) very interesting but he edits INTREPID and does have some good things in it. Also met John Knoepfle, pleasant slow-talking southerner, but dull poet. And James Wright. I was introduced to Wright as an Irish New Zealander and from that moment trouble. His greeting: "Hit someone!" Later (with no effort of any kind on my part) he initiated the following dialogue:

W: "Have you ever fought in the ring?' (belligerently).–
Me: "I don't need to fight in the ring'.–
W: "Keep you voice down!'–
Me: "I will...'–
W: "KEEP YOUR VOICE DOWN:'–
Me: "I will...until I need to raise it'."

At that point I learned that the guy was bugged because some student there had told him his Summer school course was dullsville, so I tried to placate him and be pleasant. Finally, as he was hauled away by our host, he claimed that my affability was a way of laughing at him.

Apart from such, my chief feeling while away was of the sheer hypocrisy of many American intellectuals. People who can switch on, gladhand you and switch off again before you are really out of sight.

Things are slow just now. I have three quarters of the material for a good issue of TUATARA, but had been waiting for stuff to come to me. Now woken up to the fact that if I want to shape the situation I'll have to go get it. Small point: would you object if I used also the other smaller piece of Ponge, "To Dream Substance", which is in your last letter? I like it. The Jouve by itself seems too slight perhaps to go with. I have your Celan issue (a few days ago) but no time yet to be into it.

En route from Buff I picked up a copy of Diane de Prima's MEMOIRS OF A BEATNIK, which grabbed me OK. Now into Malcolm X's autobiog. A very fine moving thing.

A note from Daphne says she is on the point of moving to Wisconsin. This afternoon an old correspondent of yours (and new acquaintance of mine), P.K. Page, is calling here. Ananasi in Toronto have shown initial interest in doing the first seven sections of my Earth Meditations poem wh I swear by (the other six sections are of the same in character as the one you saw)....

Peace, and love to you both,

Mike

Letter 33

Utano
10th August 1969

dear Mike,
Ironic about Wright, since he is presented as a sort of saintly figure by some. But he sounds a bit like Jim Dickey — with fearful violence impending. He sounds ready for the looney bin. But your answers were taking his words too directly and should have met HIS problem at root — if conversation was to mesh at all. Not simple.

The Ponge you have in your mitts is yours, of course. The Jouve was more of a checkback on the other you mentioned.

Malcolm X's book a good one and instructive. He was an exact contemporary of mine and I'm sure I saw him at least once in Boston when he was shining shoes at Roseland — for I frequented that area at that time. A sad book. Just when he was ready to be a mensch he was killed by his own people. It tells eloquently — without intending to — that the negro movement, granted success, will not in itself appreciably alter the American fantasia.

I have an appointment at U of Cal (La Jolla) for Oct of next year and I'll be in Ottawa (Carleton U) from just after Thanksgiving to the Xmas break.[20] I'd probably bus to Vancouver IF it could be made economically feasible — but I have neither money nor energy to extend myself otherwise in that direction (it represents a detour). I'll be available, it seems, about — say — the 10th or so of Nov of next year. A reading and conversation ok. NO PARTIES. And I'd rather talk with fewer people and the community at large than simply students.

PK Page and I did correspond a little some years ago. But her most recent writing — after a long layoff — not impressive.
Love always,

Cid

[20] Corman went to Ottawa through his connection with Canadian poet Raymond Souster.

LETTER 34

Utano
11th September 1969

dear Mike,

rather depressed: a note from [Paul] Celan's publishers that they are going to take action against me for doing his work. The sadness of it: that one's heartfelt and hardwon labors get stymied by such petty malevolence — that doesnt even know what it is doing. Only too typical perhaps. Not that much can come of such action, if anything — but that it is started at all.

But your MEDITATIONS (the fragments, of course, hurt consecutive reading to some extent) in and read now. There is intelligence and thought involved, but the kind of thing that doesnt convince me finally. I want a particular voice. And too much is facile.

Even Olson's new MAXies get on the nerves, get tedious — repeat. I dont take harangue well. But his problems are not yours. Only that he feels the need for some vast work — in fact, small.

Someone just sent me a copy of Borges' essays and his thing is to make a shambles of the human propensity to weave itself, to aggravate a density by complexity, confusion. Not unnaturally the cover uses a moebius strip. Actually a drawing [by] Albers — unresolvable to the eye — would have been better.

Still — I'm grateful to you for being willing to let me see. for I am interested and find points of interest. Splicings — though some of the quotes are ok in and of themselves — are likely as poetry to go flat/dead — for a voice, an underlying music of thought/feeling, is wanted. The center from which. But I know how such things go. And it is good that you have done this, have made such an effort — even if only, of course, to abandon it finally — like everything else. What stays will need no word of mine.

Your piece reminds me again that, in the face of the modern cry that we no longer have any common traditions to which to turn, modern poets especially — more than ever before — allude to a range of items that is astonishing and that demand footnoting. (This is not said in disparagement — though I've made an effort NOT to be literary or topical — unless the context is at once transcendant — myself. Rather to point up certain problems. Clayton E, for example, is perhaps even more personal and literary than Duncan; and in some ways it is ironic. Something of the fashionable gets involved.)

The weather turning slowly: and the crickets and other night insects make a dimmer dazing music of themselves. The pang in all things, in all selves.

Love always,

Cid –

LETTER 35

Victoria
September 15, 1969

Dear Cid:

Am sad and astonished at the Celan business and hope only that it was not instigated by Celan himself.

Beyond that I have some small news you may welcome. My boss has given me the go-ahead to ask you to read here in November of next year. The fee would be standard (i.e. $150). I explained that you would be coming from San Francisco and he said we could find you a fare, too. I hope all this is OK and we can perhaps make specific arrangements. At any rate, I wrote to Robin Blaser and Warren Tallman saying you would probably be here then. No reply from Blaser, but Tallman writes: "We would very much like to have Cid Corman here. But same old dumb story at the moment. No bread. But I'll talk to the dept. chairman. My guess is he might at most be able to get $100 for preferably a noon-hour possibly an evening reading. Considering all Cid has done for people here and other places should be a lot more...Anyway let me know when and if plans for Cid shape up'.

As you know, I expected your reaction to my EARTH MEDS to be somewhat as is, though I won't say I'm not disappointed. The thing is, I can accept your view of the poem completely, because I know that in my own way there is some sense in which I share you response to things. I can throw it back at you this way. You finish: "The pang in all things, in all selves'. Now, I don't know you (if only that we have not yet met in person). Few people, it seems to me, could write a sentence like that and get across the intensity of meaning in it that you do. I appreciate that. What you say there is at the core of my own reaction to the world as is. So, I feel you are right too about my poem. But I stay with it, too, because it is as right for me as any poem I can now make could be.

To return, momentarily, to Celan. I don't know quite why, but it doesn't greatly engage me. Certainly I haven't yet paid enough attention, but what I have yields a solemn (and diluted?) Morgenstern. Or am I just talking like a horse's ass and not at all on the wave-length?

We too have fall, red leaf and rising winds and last night sun setting, a clear ball, hardedged, amethyst.

Love to you both, and peace,

Mike

LETTER 36

Utano
22nd September 1969

dear Mike,

yes, I'm afraid Celan himself has worked the whole thing up
singlehanded. I don't expect anything to come of it, but sad anyhow
— that he is so slow to see/realize that my labors as well as intentions
are of the best. And I have been utterly open with him throughout.
(Actually if I didnt myself send him a copy, he would never have
known of the issue.)

Celan has no relation I know of to Morgenstern. More to Goll
and Mandelstam. His harrowing youth in concentration camps and
the death of his parents in that scene has left a gory trail and a constant
ache in his work. But he knows how to make language move and live
— and what he does is a stimulus. As some have already realized.
However, he is not easy and he does get awfully dismal.

Thank you for wanting me there. And I hope it will bring us
nearer. My word on anything is no more than that. No one will ever
read you with the same care that went into your work.

Love always,

Cid

LETTER 37

Utano
11th January 1970

Dear Mike,

Word today that Olson is dying, perhaps of cancer, in NY hospital. What can anyone do? He's lent himself to it, long since. Perhaps since the death of his 2nd wife. His work as a teacher remains. Without his voice and personality behind the work something will be lost. But he's influenced a generation.

Dear Phyllis [Webb] — I havent seen her for 15 years! Since London. Roy [Kiyooka] you likely would enjoy and he does know the scene there very well....

The poems not convincing — though the effort ok. To come in as those pieces do — between Creeley and myself (largely) — is to require a decidedly precise voice. Not a literary approach. But short poems harder than people realize. Harder, in fact, than a 10p poem.

Here we seem to be coming out of our flu bug into the light of coming day — or so I hope. It has been a not very auspicious opening to the year.

Love always,

Cid

LETTER 38

Feb 26, 1970
Victoria, B.C.

Dear Cid,

Tuatara came out a few days ago, so I am getting 2 copies off to you, though at present impeded by a mild 'flu & a (mild) bout of overwork. I am beginning already to put materials together for nos 3 & 4, & shall send mss. for No.2 to Victor next week....

Olson is dead, then. The way of things. Now I suppose the academic floodgates begin to open.

As to printing — if I seemed to wonder about Victor's reliability I gave a mistaken impression. I have no real impression at all of VC yet. In April I am reading in Toronto & I'll be staying with him then. As far as that goes, I simply wanted to get an idea of the costs of Japanese printing....I suppose I could deal direct with a Japanese printer if it was financially feasible. My real reason for enquiring is that I admire the fastidiousness of much of the work I've seen....

Alas, I am becoming used to your finding my poems unconvincing. So be it. So be it. I guess you wd. need to see a great welter of the stuff. Even then, though, you wd. not be "convinced". I feel as if I have learnt much from yourself, & Bob Creeley, but my temperament differs (apparently) from both of yours. I mean, quite an area of my work is as near to someone like Bukowski as to anything. I don't imagine you wd. go for that. Yet one can't deny the realities of oneself. I do see, by the way, that I am more "literary' than either RC or yourself. This is in part a fault, but also partly natural (for better or worse) — my own "academic" side....

Love to you both,

Mike

Utano
9th June 1969

dear Mike,
                rather than impose on your
space—let me just send this one Ponge
piece - a very charming one - which I
believe has never been done before.

        If you decide to use it, as I hope
you will, let me know and I'll send you
Ponge's address—so that you can send him
a copy or two when the issue appears.

        If you would like a little
more, let me know also—but be clear. And
if you dont want this, please let me have it
back, for it is a better version than any I
have here and I can use it in ORIGIN.

        (I have no copy of it.)

        love.

        always

67

LETTER 39

Utano
3rd March 1970

dear Mike,

Dont be dismayed by my response to your work. Obviously it reflects precisely where you are, etc. And there is no way to hasten one's life — or not to any sensible purpose. More vital — whatever it may seem or sound like — I am quite sympathetic. I've enjoyed much of Bukowski's work — but feel no call to return to it after the initial hearing/look. and anyone can see in ORIGIN that my taste is not confined by any means to poets whose work resembles my own.

You'll probably meet Ray Souster in Toronto — an old and trusted friend of mine — and perhaps some others that I know. I've always had warm relations there. I hope and expect it will go well with you.

Love always,
Cid

LETTER 40

Utano
22nd April 1970

Dear Mike —

fine. Your previous letter sounded a bit unhappy about my contribution. And I dont want you to feel pressured.

Pleased that N[ew]D[irections] is sending you a copy of the book — though I'd personally prefer NO reviews. Perhaps John Taggart — since he is becoming an expert on the subject — wd take it on, however. (He has a copy already.) Main thing is—actually—that he is someone you should be in contact with and this may set it up.

No—nothing on CO. The letter of CO's you refer to is an early one that comes after I had expressed doubts that he was quite the hotshot that RC had made out. RC HAD come on awfully strong and CO had opened with a powerploy — quite characteristic but NEW to me — and my response was also characteristic: I dont cotton to pressure of any kind. His answer, however, made me realize that he had more on the ball than could be doubted. And his work was exciting.

I wish some of my letters were available of that time. Not that they wouldnt reveal weaknesses, but also show certain aspects of the relationship not otherwise clear. I dont know, however, that they now exist. (If he was intelligent, he should have sold them, for they were worth as much in cash as his own: though, in fact, his letters between us were livelier.)

I havent seen the book as yet.

Nor have I seen Dorn's GUNSLINGER— though several people have written me of it warmly. I'll catch up when I'm 'back'.

For reasons that I cant follow, people in Vancouver area prefer to keep me in the dark about engagements that must be decided by now. Unless clarity comes soon, I'll give up that leg of the journey. I dont have clear word from Victoria either. I want to know dates (roughly) and pay. All the word I receive is indirect.

But I would like to see you.

And hope that TUATARA will grow.

Love always,
Cid

LETTER 41

Victoria
April 27, 1970

Dear Cid:

Yours in today. The 'clear word' you get from Victoria will be from me. Thing is, I have been waiting on you. To give me exact dates when you want to be here. Then I would write you the "official" note etc. Or do you want me to name dates. Whichever way you like. As soon as a date is fixed for you to read/talk then the whole thing can be settled. It now rests with me, you see.

Oddly enough I had a note a few days ago fm a guy unknown to me, Ron Silliman, mentioning Taggart (and his mag Maps). I have now writ JT a note, but have only the most generalized address (Newburg, Penn) and I just hope it gets there. I have asked him as you suggested and have greedily not mentioned that ND are sending me a copy of LIVINGDYING.

I have never been able to find Ponge's address and I wd like him to get your TUATARA pieces as, I agree, they are certainly beautiful. I would be happy to have more (though I appear now to be full until this time next year). Very happy, in fact, and wd squeeze them in or fatten the mag for their sake. Do you like Michaux, by the way, and, if so, have you ever done any? Also any Japanese people (don't know if I mentioned, I have had FROGS AND OTHERS for some time).

Have put aside the ORIGIN letters just now. Most intriguing. That glowing start, to the gap and then formality of the closing letter. Yes, I certainly hope yr part of the corresp. is available somewhere.

Peace, and much love,

Mike –

LETTER 42

Utano
2nd May 1970

dear Mike,

....Evidently you dont know ORIGIN very well: Michaux was wellrepresented in the 1st series and I had a large chunk from one of his drug books in Ferlinghetti's shortlived JOURNAL. (I've met Michaux: a fine person and like his work.)[21]

....TUATARA has something going and anyone who fails to sense it reveals himself as feeble of wit. So. With or without grass, hope you stay well and busy.

Love always,
Cid

---

[21] Doyle had written to Corman asking him if he was familiar with the work of Michaux.

Dear Cid:

Am sad and astonished at the Celan business and hope only that it was not instigated by Celan himself.

Beyond that I have some small news you may welcome. My boss has given me the go-ahead to ask you to read here in November of next year. The fee would be standard (i.e. $150). I explained that you would be coming from San Francisco and he said we could find you a fare, too. I hope all this is OK and we can perhaps make specific arrangements. At any rate, I wrote to Robin Blaser and Warren Tallman saying you would probably be here then. No reply from Blaser, but Tallman writes: "We would very much like to have Cid Corman here. But same old dumb story at the moment. No bread. But i'll talk to the dept. chairman. My guess is he might at most be able to get $100 for preferably a noon-hour possibly an evening reading. Considering all Cid has done for people here and other places should be a lot more...Anyway let me know when and if plans for Cid shape up".

As you know, I expected your reaction to my EARTH MEDS to be somewhat as is, though I won't say I'm not disappointed. The thing is, I can accept your view of the poem completely, because I know that in my own way there is some sense in which I share your response to things. I can throw it back at you this way. You finish: "The pang in all things, in all selves". Now, I feel real friendship for you and yet there is an obvious sense in which I don't know you (if only that we have not yet met in person). Few people, it seems to me, could write a sentence like that and get across the intensity of meaning it that you do. I appreciate that. What you say there is at the core of my own reaction to the world as is. So, I feel you are right too about my poem. But I stay with it, too, because it is as right for me as any poem I can now make could be.

There is another poet here just now, Robert Sward. I like some of his work and he is a gentle, sensitive fellow (though with a certain flair and flamboyance of his own). I told him how I hope to get you to come here next year and the possibility greatly appeals to him. He expresses great respect for your work, and this pleases me too.

Teaching year started today. Met three classes. Can only say that, as usual, the people seemed young and fresh and good. But what else? This is life. And on it goes.

Not sure I want to continue with Caterpillar, but I probably shall though is a long way from the mags CE names his models. There are always one or two good things. Also in a mag called Wormwood Review. To return, momentarily, Celan. I don't know quite why, but it doesn't greatly engage me. Certainly haven't yet paid enough attention, but what I have yields a solemn (and luted?) Morgenstern. Or am I just talking like a horse's ass and not at all the wavelength?

We too have fall, red leaf and rising winds and last night sun setting, a ear ball, hardedged, amethyst.

Love to you both, and peace, *Mike*

LETTER 43

Victoria
May 11, 1970

Dear Cid:

....Strange stuff from this Silliman, really. It is spread around the page, but doesn't really create a field of energy. When the 'lines' are put in more conventional arrangement they don't have a great deal.

My experience has great gaps. No, I am not very familiar with the first series of ORIGIN. Being in NZ. Probably for same reason that you haven't yet seen GUNSLINGER.

Jim Weil wrote me a good generous glowing letter the other day about TUATARA. As it comes from him, I feel considerably encouraged by it. Have just been re-reading TROPIC OF CANCER and BLACK SPRING for courses next year. I first read COLOSSUS AT MAROUSSI twenty years ago and find still the same sense of M's vitality and courage. Yr own work, by the way, is included in that same course (for what these things are usually worth. Not very damn much. Though this course will set out to be deliberately 'subjective' and will have a picked small bunch of A and B students, some of whom have asked to enrol already and look promisingly unsquare.)

Peace,

Mike

Letter 44

Utano
15th May 1970

dear Mike,

about 4 months from the time you receive this we set forth. The pace seems fast already. #20 will go to the printers by the 1st of June and that (hopefully) lets me out.

Your formal invitation appreciated and that makes that clear: we will meet and on your home ground. Which is, or course, best. No word yet from Vancouver — but the one date with you already makes a visit feasible. We can work out the details at least a month in advance.

My approach is always informal. I assume there wont be more than 35-50 people there interested and that may give me a chance to talk with them more. I hope too that the 50 minutes can be exceeded — if the feeling warrants.

My approach to students is radically different from anyone else's I know. completely OPEN: i.e., no goals and no texts in advance. But that's a thing in itself. Though it connects closely with my work....

My own poetry you will find also moves in a particular way when voiced.

It seems like I'm destined to arrive at a very lively moment in America — just when US elections will be in the offing, the first polit- ical responses to Nixon's tenure. (I expect 'results' to be, as usual, inconclusive — but I have many people to meet and discuss issues with — yourself happily included.)

Love always,

Cid –

LETTER 45

La Jolla
30 Oct 70

Dear Mike,
all sounds ok. I'll be in Vancouver, coming by air, on the 11th probably — or early afternoon of the 12th. Probably leave Victoria on the 14th and fly to Milwaukee. The weekend is for Lorine Niedecker — a meeting we've looked forward to for many years. I wish it were less hurried, but...

Love always,
Cid —

POETRY READING C I D   C O R M A N
Friday, November 13 at 8 p.m. in MacLaurin 111

CID CORMAN is well-known as poet, editor and translator. His magazine Origin, the first to publish consistently the work of Charles Olson, Robert Creeley and others, is the founding magazine of the Black Mountain movement and is one of the truly important poetry magazines of the twentieth-century. Many volumes of Corman's poetry have been published, including Words for Each Other (London, 1968) and Livingdying (New York: New Directions, 1970). His work has appeared in leading literary magazines (both in English and translation) in many parts of the world. He has also done very fine translations of a number of contemporary French poets and of Japanese and German poetry.

Cid Corman lives in Kyoto, Japan, and this is his first trip to North America in a long time. With his wife, he is travelling to many parts of the United States and Canada, giving talks and readings. Happily, UVic is on his Canadian schedule.

Persons Referred To And Manner of Reference
(Unless otherwise noted, the individuals listed are American poets)

Albers: Albers, Josef: Amerian painter
Alexander, D: D Alexander
Allen, Donald M.: Don Allen: American editor and anthologist
Arnett, Carroll: Carroll Arnett

Baxter, James K.: Baxter, New Zealand poet
Beckett, Samuel: Beckett: Irish playwright and novelist
Berg, Leila: educationist
Berge, Carol: Carol Berge
Blackburn, Paul: PB
Blaser, Robin: Blaser
Bly, Robert: Bly
Bronk, William: Bronk, Bill Bronk
Bukowski, Charles: Bukowski
Bunting, Basil: Bunting: English poet

Candelaria, Fred: Fred Candelaria, musician, poet, editor
Carruth, Hayden: Carruth
Celan, Paul: Celan, German poet
Challis, Gordon: New Zealand poet and translator
Cohen, Leonard: Len Cohen, Canadian poet and songwriter
Coleman, Victor: Victor Coleman, Canadian poet and editor
Creeley, Robert: RC, Creeley
Curnow, Allen: Curnow, New Zealand poet, playwright, and editor

Daive, Jean: unnamed reference, French poet
Daumal, Rene: Daumal, French poet
DeLoach, Allen: editor
DiPrima, Diane: Diane DiPrima
Dickey, James: JDickey, Dickey
Dorn, Ed: Ed Dorn
DuBouchet, André: DuBouchet, French poet
Duncan, Robert: RD, Duncan
Dunlop, Lane: Lane Dunlop

Eigner, Larry: Larry Eigner
Emmanuel, Pierre: Pierre Emmanuel
Enslin, Theodore: Ted Enslin, Enslin
Eshelman, Clayton: Clayton E, CE

Ferlinghetti, Lawrence: Ferlinghetti
Frost, Robert: Frost

Gascoyne, David: Gascoyne, English poet
Ghose, Zulfikar: Zulfikar Ghose, Pakistani novelist and poet
Goll, Yvan: Goll, French poet

H.D. (Hilda Doolittle): HD
Hecht, Roger: Hecht
Holt, John: Holt, educationist

Johnson, Louis: Johnson, New Zealand poet
Jouve, Pierre Jean: PJJ, Jouve, French poet

Kearns, Lionel: Canadian poet
Keller, Dean, librarian
Kelly, Robert
Kiyooka, Roy: Roy Kiyooka, Canadian poet, visual artist, editor
Knoeppfle, John: John Knoepfle

Levertov, Denise: DL, Denny Levertov
Levi-Strauss: Claude, Levi-Strauss, French Anthropologist
Logan, John: Logan
Lowell, Robert: Lowell

Mandelstam, Osip: Mandelstam, Russian poet
Marlatt: Daphne Marlatt, Canadian poet
Marshall, Lenore: Lenore
McGilvery, Lawrence: LM, McGilvery, bookseller
Merwin, W.S.: Merwin
Michaux, Henri: Michaux, French poet
Miller, Henry: American novelist

Morgenstern, Christian: Morgenstern, German poet

Niedecker, Lorine: Lorine, LN

Olson, Charles: Olson, CO

Page, P.K.: Canadian poet
Pearson, Norman Holmes: NHP, Pearson, American professor
Perchik, Simon: Perchik
Perls, Fritz: Perls, psychologist
Ponge, Francis: FP, Ponge
Pound, Ezra: EP, Pound, Ezra

Quinn, Sister M. Bernetta: American critic

Rago, Henry: Rago
Randall, Margaret: Margaret Randall, Meg Randall
Rothenberg, Jerome: Rothenberg

Sanders, Ed: Ed Sanders
Sankey, John: Sankey, English editor and printer
Seidman,Hugh: Seidman
Silliman, Ron: Silliman
Snyder, Gary: Snyder, Gary
Souster, Raymond: Ray Souster, Canadian poet
Spicer, Jack: Spicer
Stafford, William: William Stafford
Stevens, Holly: Holly, American scholar and editor
Stevens, Wallace: WS, Stevens
Swenson, May: May Swenson

Taggart, John: Taggart
Tallman, Warren: Tallman, American editor and essayist
Tarn, Nathaniel: Tarn, English editor and poet
Thomas, Edward: Edward Thomas, British poet
Tomlinson, Charles: Tomlinson, English poet

Wakoski, Diane: Wakoski, DW

Weaver, Mike: English scholar
Webb, Phyllis: Phyllis Webb, Phyllis, Canadian poet
Weil, James L.: Jim Weil
Whalen, Phillip: Phil Whalen
Whitney, J.D.: J.D. Whitney
Wieners, John: Wieners
Wilbur, Richard: Dick Wilbur
Williams, Florence Herman: Floss, Flossie
Williams, William Carlos: WCW, Bill
Woolf, Douglas: Doug Woolf
Wright, James: Wright

Zukofsky, Louis: LZ, Louis, Zukofsky

TUATARA

759 Helvetia Crescent,
Victoria, B.C.
Canada.

Editor: Mike Doyle

30 June 1974

Dear Cid,

Good, & appropriate, to have these poems of yours close the last issue of this series. When (& if) I begin again I'd like to do a mag in collaboration with one or two other writers.

I'll send you a batch of my own poems before too long. At the moment I'm having difficulty in finding a publisher for a book of short poems, & am pretty heavily into my WCW criticism book for Routledge.

We go to NZ in October for 4½ months, & I hope to be freer there for a while & perhaps more communicative.

Kindest regards to you & to Shizumi,

Mike Doyle

AFTERWORD

Reading these letters thirty years later is salutary and chastening. To this day, I remain an admirer of the purity and economy of Cid's poetry, though I have not found it of a kind I can emulate while remaining true to myself.

To Cid's work as editor and critic I have a more complicated response. The various series of **Origin** provide an admirable literary legacy, most particularly in the austerity and good judgement of the early series. But, from the very beginning, given Cid's criteria for poetry—so much in evidence in the correspondence above—there are anomalies. To take one obvious example: I have long admired the best of Irving Layton's poetry, but how does Cid Corman, purist and minimalist, come to feature the work of a poet so rhetorical and so formally conventional?

With regard to my own work, Cid gave good advice, for which I continue to be grateful. At the moment of this writing, we remain friends, although there have been long gaps in our correspondence. Was Cid's advice right for me? On the whole, it was useful and revealing, though I have never fully met his rigorous specifications. Rather, I have found myself in the area of James Wright, a poet Cid tends to reject. Much more to the point, our long exchange of letters has provided friendship, encouragement, and a unifying sense of the larger world of poetry.

In the whole living of his life, Cid Corman has epitomized poetry in my generation. Admiring him and thanking him for that, I am grateful for my small part of it.

Mike Doyle
July 1999–

FOUR WITHOUT NECKS   (after Desnos)

who kept their heads no longer.
Four with their necks snapped,
call them the neckless four.

When they drank a glass
in a café on the square or boulevard
the boys didn't forget to bring some funnels.

When they ate it was bloody,
all four sang and sobbed.
When they loved, it was their own blood.

When they ran, it was of wind.
When they wept, it was for living.
When they slept, it was without regret.

TUATARA

759 Helvetia Crescent,
Victoria, B.C.
Canada.

Editor: Mike Doyle

26 Feb 1974

Dear Cid,

Good to have your letter a month or so ago, & your response
to Tuatara # 11, sensitive as always.

Since #12 is to be the last in this series, I wonder if you
would like to contribute work to it? Would, of course, be
delighted to have some. Apart from the usual crop of new
people I have good work for it from Bob Creeley, Larry Eigner
and Jerry Rothenberg. I am writing today to see if Robert
Duncan would like to send something, though I've not heard
from him since he was here three years ago.

I am now pretty well free of the university politics. The
scene does get me down from time to time & it is the usual
bad academic scene in any case, but somehow it comes to me
as something to fight back against.

I have been writing, though rather sporadically, & soon am
on leave during which I hope to really get back to full spate.
My "official" job for that leave is to do a book on WCW for
Routledge.

I hesitate to send you my work, since I feel that it isn't
of a kind you like. Though I do have a little book which
is coming out right now in Toronto & I'll send you that when
copies turn up.

I've wanted to do a biggish book of short poems for some time,
but can't think who to send them to, having no "ins" here even
yet especially. Somewhat over a year ago I send Jim Weil a
ms of selected poems going back to the mid-fifties. He didn't
like it. Nevertheless (& it says a lot for both of us!) we
seem, though we have never met, to have a bond of sympathy,
a related "feel" for things. Perhaps I should have tried
him with a book of only recent work, but I guess it wd be
too eclectic.

Even in such quiescent locations as this, life is somehow
a welter of this & that, but we do not forget you both there.

Good peace,

Mike Doyle

28th July 82

Dear Mike —

Thanks for writing. The situation is dreadful. But somehow we'll work it out (soon) & most likely return to Japan no later than next spring & possibly by New Year's.

My Australian contacts are mostly unhappy ones: Clive Faust & Jan Kasarcot(?) — Watson (latter of LaTrobe Univ — Phil. Dept — in Bundoora): They are good friends. He may you may know better than I do. People in N.Z. otherwise: & That's your province. I'd like to see yr. work on new & old — cheap editions. Best to wait on my next move also. But always happy to see poetry of yours (beyond critique).

#20 shd. be out in Sept. Finally, done inside it.

Victoria NOT seriously though: it was near an unusual opportunity. Love to you both

always —

Cid Corman was born in Roxbury, Massachusetts in 1924. He is a poet, editor of the journal, *Origin*, owner of the Origin Press, editor and translator of the work of several other poets, and literary critic. As editor of Origin Press for nearly 50 years, Corman has published — if not debuted — some of the seminal poets of the 20th century: Olson, Creeley, Eigner, Bronk, Enslin, Niedecker, Zukofsky, Snyder. The author of over a hundred books, Corman is also a translator of many ancients and moderns, such as as translator of poets from Japan, Italy, France, etc., among them André du Bouchet, Philippe Jaccottet, René Char, Antonin Artaud, Apollinaire, Baudelaire, Rimbaud, Mallarmé, and more recently, Henri-Simon Faure, Alain Malherbe and Laurent Grisel. Corman, who has lived mostly in Japan since 1954, received the Lenore Marshall Poetry Prize in 1974. An energetic and devoted correspondent, his letters are postmarked "Kyoto, Japan."

Mike Doyle, whose background is Irish,Mike Doyle, whose background is Irish, grew up in London, England, and has lived in Canada for just on thirty years. He has received a UNESCO International Writers' Fellowship, and fellowships from the Canada Council, the American Council of Learned Societies, and the Social Sciences and Humanities Research Council. He has published several books of poems, most recently *Trout Spawning at Lardeau River* and *Intimate Absences: Selected Poems*, and was the editor of the defunct literary magazine *Tuatara*. He has written books on William Carlos Williams and James K. Baxter, and a biography of Richard Aldington, plus critical essays on William Carlos Williams, Wallace Stevens, H.D., Irving Layton, Alfred Purdy, and others. He has also written and taught on links between modern poetry and the visual arts. His home is in Victoria, .B.C., and he spends the winter in Mexico

Kegan Doyle, the editor of *Where to Begin: the Selected Letters of Cid Corman and Mike Doyle*, was born in Auckland, New Zealand, and raised in Victoria, B.C. Kegan Doyle has a PhD from the University of Toronto and currently teaches at the University of British Columbia in Vancouver.

WHERE TO BEGIN

AGMV Marquis

MEMBRE DU GROUPE SCABRINI

Québec, Canada
2000